You Got This! Letters to a Single Mom

Alexis Kennedy

BookLeaf Publishing

India | USA | UK

Presentation by *BookLeaf Publishing*

Web: www.bookleafpub.com

E-mail: info@bookleafpub.com

ISBN: 9789358315172

First edition 2024

*To Camyrn, you are a gift and I am grateful to
be your mom. I love you.*

ACKNOWLEDGEMENT

Thank you to my book coach Charissa for making me write when I wanted to quit.

And to everyone who told me in one way or another, "I see you." You helped me keep going.

To the "Village," thank you.

PREFACE

I didn't start off as a single mom. My then-husband and I decided within a year of our matrimony that, though we were young, we wanted a child. The marriage didn't make it but out of it came a beautiful baby girl and me, a single mom trying to figure this thing out and raise her while still trying to raise myself. I heard a phrase by Gretchen Rubin that says, "The days are long but the years are short." Now that she's 17, that has proven true. I look back and don't really know where the time went but when I look at my letters and journals, I know it took a lot of tears, selflessness, encouragement, affirmation, prayers and late night cookie dough to get through it.

To the other single moms like me, I don't have all the answers but I do know that every day we wake up and get out of bed and just keep trying, we show our babies that anything is possible. I pray this book blesses you, encourages you and lets you know we see you! We are rooting for you. Keep going!

Shout out to you, Single Mom

You, who shows up for the little one every day. You, who shows up in every way, even when you're tired. Even when the snooze button on the alarm clock says, "No! Sleep in today; take a little minute for now."
Shout to you, we say, "Thank you."

You, the one who hastily leaves her job to pick up your kids from school when they're sick and rubs their belly to make them feel better.

You have to be the one who chases away the monsters under the bed and reads the bedtime story when you would rather be alone in your bed. You, the one who stays up with them when they're having a bad dream; you who dries the tears.

You patch up the boo-boos, find a way to get them to take medicine even when they don't want to, cook and do the laundry. You keep up with every schedule and appointment, show up to baseball games in your work clothes but at least you make it.

Thank you.
Shout out to you single mom for all the time you wondered how you were gonna make it; you didn't give up and somehow you made it through. Shout out to you single mom for all the times you would cry yourself to sleep hoping your kids wouldn't hear.

You, for making sure the tank had gas and making sure the refrigerator had food. Even if there was none for yourself.
Shout out to you single mom for watching your kids make cartwheels on the floor and show you all of their latest drawings when all you wanted to do was literally nothing at all but you never let them see it.

Shout out to you, single mom, for all the time you didn't get a break, didn't get a rest, didn't get vacation and couldn't find a sitter, couldn't go on a date but you never let the kids see you upset. Thank you.

Shout out to you for every practice, every rehearsal you fought traffic to chauffeur them to. Thank you, that even when you have a reason, a real good one too, to trash down their father, you chose silence. Thank you for being the comfort. Thank you for the discipline.

Thank you for not giving in.
Thank you for not throwing in the towel.
Thank you for not giving up without a fight.
Thank you for your strength.
Thank you.

For every seed you sowed to persevere, you may
not see the fruit now but one day you will. One
day you will see your children rising up and
standing up, becoming greater than you dreamed
or imagined. They watched their mother rise up
and stand. And you kept standing when
obstacles came your way. You kept standing
when life made you want to tap out. You stood
for them and kept standing.

You are strong. You are capable. You are
enough.
You, single mom, with your two arms to protect
that baby, to provide for that baby, to nurture
that baby.
You did it.
Shout out to you, Single mom.
To you we say, "Thank you."

On Days You Are Just Glad You Make It Through

Hey Incredible Mom (that's you!),

Isn't it crazy how fast 24 hours go by?
Just for today let's not look at what you didn't
accomplish.
Let's not look at the load of laundry.
Let's not look at the dishes in the sink. Let's not
look at that toy on the floor.

For today give yourself a round of applause for
what you did accomplish.
You faced the day head on, and even though
there may still be some things on your To Do
List you missed, you crushed the day by making
it through!

You made it to the finish line, even if all you did
today was tell your babies you love them.
You did enough!
So for today give yourself a pat on the back. For
today, stand in that mirror and say, "Well done."
For today, put your feet up and say, "You go
girl." You didn't let this day overtake you, so
even in that you won.

"Today I gave my 100%. That may not look like yesterday's 100% but for today it was enough. Tomorrow I'll wake with purpose and strength to give that day all I've got but for today I am proud of me. I gave my all and that's enough."

On the days you aren't feeling strong….

Hey you amazing mom you,
I know you may not feel like it today.
Maybe the worries of the day got you down.
Maybe it was trying to be in multiple places at multiple times, or having to pour out so much that you thought was in your capacity. But hear me when I say this: you are strong.

YOU ARE CAPABLE. YOU ARE EQUIPPED.

You have all the wisdom you need inside of you to know how to get it all done and when to get it all done. YOU ARE STRONG.

Yes, the pressures of life come. But you CAN handle them, just like you have handled them countless times before. YOU ARE STRONG! You may be down, but you are not out! YOU ARE STRONG!

Your track record shows that you, yes YOU, ARE undefeated. Tired, yes, but undefeated. Maybe feeling a little weak, but STILL UNDEFEATED. Maybe searching for answers, but undefeated. You, my dear, are strong and you have everything you need to conquer and rise.

And you got little eyes counting on you to push through, to not give up. The fact that you guys are still here despite every obstacle and every tear that came your way before today shows that you are unstoppable. YOU ARE STRONG and I believe the best is still yet to come!

"I AM A CHAMPION. I have climbed every mountain that ever came my way and I'll climb this one too. I am strong. I am a warrior and the scars of life can't stop me; they just add more kinks to my armor. Because I am unstoppable! Problems can't break me. Disappointment can't shake me. Because I'm a champion and I'm strong."

On Days You're Feeling Stuck...

Hey Magnificent Mommy,

I get it. It's hard trying to have all the answers. Sometimes you look at the road ahead, where you are wanting to go, wanting to do, wanting to have…. And it all just seems light years away.

Take heart in this: you're closer today than you were a month ago; you're closer today than you were a year ago.
You're not stuck on your journey. You're just at a stop sign and stop signs are temporary!
Stop signs allow us to pause and check the GPS to make sure we're going in the right direction. Heart check!

Stop signs allow us to change the radio station to make sure we've got the right frequency in our ears, the right encouraging words, the right affirmations, the "yes you can do it," not the "girl, give up" playing in the background.

Stop signs allow us to quickly check the back seat or passenger seat to make sure our little ones are OK. In other words, if you feel stuck today, it's a good place to pause and reflect on just how far you've come on your journey—even if it was just an inch.

You're doing great! Keep going! Those inches will become miles someday! Eventually you'll be able to look back and say, "wow, I did it."

If you're feeling stuck today, know that it is not forever. This is the place to pause, reflect, shift, pivot, meditate, give thanks for the little things.

And then tomorrow we get up and try again. Stuck doesn't mean forever. Tomorrow could be the day you get unstuck, the day you wake up with more energy, the day you wake up with a new plan, the day you wake up with a new strategy,
the day you wake up and realize you've got resources right there all along, you just had to uncover them.

Today happened. Tomorrow, you wake up and put a new brick towards the foundation you're building. Tomorrow we get unstuck.

"I am not my circumstances. I'm not staying in this place, I'm just passing through. There's

greater in store for me, greater opportunities, greater resources, greater relationships, a great plan and a great breakthrough. In fact I'm not stuck, I'm breaking through."

On Days When You Are Unable to Rest

Hey Momma,

It's time…it's time to turn off the TV and put down the phone and just rest.

You've done all you can do today, pacing the floor won't change a thing. Binge watching something watch-worthy on Netflix sounds appealing, but tonight my prayer list is that you rest.

I pray that as you pull the covers up, you are blanketed with peaceful thoughts, thoughts of your kids laughter, your favorite dessert, or hey even a memory of the last goodnight sleep you had. I pray that your sleep tonight trumps that one, that there is no tossing, there's no turning. Just a sweet melody of goodness in your ears and in your mind.

I pray that as you're drifting off to sleep tonight you're not overwhelmed with the schedule of tomorrow but instead overwhelmed with the sweetest of dreams.

I pray that tonight you don't just sleep, you REST. I pray you wake up energized, pumped,

revitalized and restored in your heart and your
mind.
It's time, Momma.
JUST REST.

*"I can rest well tonight, knowing that rest is a
part of my superpower. Tonight, I don't just
sleep; I rest. The more I rest, the more I
replenish myself. The more I rest, the more I am
refueled to be there for them. Rest is a good
thing. Rest is necessary and I welcome the
sweetest rest in my life."*

Lexi's Sticky Note (11/20/23)

13

Yes, we are moms, but we are also humans.
It's okay to feel.....

Feel your feelings, but keep going,
Feel your feelings, but keep going.

On Days You Want to Give Up the Fight

Don't give up the fight!

Sometimes you're fighting with your past or your fears,
or your worries or your anxiety, or your kids temper tantrums,
or comparison,
or your kids' needs versus your own or the finances.
But don't give up the fight.

You can't have a victory, if you don't stay in the ring!!

"My name is Victory and I WILL win."

On Days You Forgot Your Crown...

Crown on.
Invisible though it might be.
You are Royalty.
Head up, crown on.

Crown on.
You are a queen, Royalty runs in your veins
And everyday you push forward, you show your heirs,
Your legacies, that they are royal too.
Shoulders back, crown on.

Crown on.
YOU ARE ROYALTY.
Head high.
Crown on.

On Days You are Scared to Ask for Help...

It's ok to ask for help.
I learned that late in life.
It's ok to ask for help.

"Help" doesn't mean you're not a strong independent woman and it doesn't mean you're incapable.

Help DOES mean you're wise, wise enough to know to use the human capital, the treasure of human resources available to you. Your village.

It means you are wise enough to say, "Before I exhaust myself, let me call in my village to prevent burnout."

In other words asking for help AND TAKING IT it's a beautiful human thing. If you've got people near you that you can call on, you're blessed and blessed indeed. It's OK to ask for help.

Yes, you can do it all by yourself but, momma, that doesn't mean you have to.

"One of the greatest, courageous steps I could ever take, is not taking it all on myself but being humble enough to ask for help. Yes I can do all things Yes I can handle everything but that doesn't mean I have to. I can ask for help and still be strong."

On Days of Comparison....

Just so you know—

none of us have it all together,

And none of us have it all figured out.

Most of us are hanging by a coattail at this
parenting thing or
just good at *pretending* we have it all figured
out.

Heart check: burn the social media highlight
reel.

We are all in the same boat trying to row to
shore together, so take heart today.

If you find yourself counting all the ways you
don't make the mark, STOP!
You're in good company and none of us do.
We are all putting together our own puzzle, one
piece at a time.

No one else has the child you have, so no one
else can parent like you. And spoiler alert:
You're doing great just the way you are.
In case no one else has told you today, you are
doing a great job.

*"I am the best mother I can be. I don't have to
compare myself to anyone else or equate myself
to anyone else's standards. I was assigned these
beautiful babies for a reason and I understand
my assignment to raise them healthy and strong
and I am doing just that. No competition here,
no comparison here. I am the best mother that I
can be."*

On Days You Wanna Go Off on Him

Don't take the bait!

You've come too far, and even though you might possibly feel better after you go off,

Would things actually BE any better?

You let off steam but did you get results?

You got little eyes looking up at you, expecting
you to make the best example possible of how to
handle adversity and conflict,
and so when you wanna go off, remind yourself
nobody wins that way and it's probably not
worth your time.

Go write your journal, go for a ride or a walk,
eat your favorite comfort foods and just say no!

Do not give him that validation because he
doesn't deserve it.
Do not give your kids that distraction because
they don't deserve it.

And do not give yourself that spike in your
blood pressure because you don't deserve it.

You deserve peace and your peace is your
responsibility.
You'll find a way to coparent peacefully in time
but for today they'll go off on him.

Today, even though it's hard, choose peace and
healthy communication.
I know you want to, because even as I'm writing
this I want to, but LISTEN:

DON'T TAKE THE BAIT!

*"I am in control of my emotions and my words. I
don't give him that power. I choose my words
well to get the right results. No one else but me
can control my emotions or my day. I choose
myself and my children. I choose our peace AND
our boundaries. I am stronger than this
temporary inconvenience. I choose peace."*

On the Not So Cute Days....

Even with your stretch marks, you're beautiful.
Even with food or milk stains on your blouse
you're beautiful.
Even with thinning edges, you're beautiful.

Even with bags under your eyes, you're beautiful
Even if he walked away, you're beautiful
Even with gray hair, you're beautiful.

If gravity and your breasts have had a fight and
gravity finally won and they're sagging down to
your belt loop, you're so beautiful.
Even with a few extra pounds, no matter what
the scale says, you're beautiful.

Why because you took on the charge of being a
mom which is sometimes the most thankless,
underrated, sacrificial job on the planet but
you're doing it and you're doing it well.

 And so even if you didn't put makeup on today,
even if you've worn sweatpants for an entire
month, you're still beautiful.
There could never be another you!

I know you may not feel like it today, but affirm it every day until you do.
You stand in the mirror and you say it every day until you believe it: you are beautiful.

"I am absolutely beautiful. Inside and out there's something special about me. I believe it and I know it. I'm beautiful and there's no one else like me. I AM BEAUTIFUL!"

Lexi's Sticky Note 12/1/2023

24

Feel, Deal, Heal.

Feel your feelings because they are valid. Cry, yell, scream, get it out.

Deal with them by coming up with a reasonable solution. How did I get here? How do I move on from here?

Heal. Move forward in peace, grateful for what you learned.

Feel, Deal, Heal.

On Days the Finances are Low...

I can remember our lowest season, when I
counted the number of hot dogs that come in a
pack
and the number of slices that come in a sleeve of
bread and calculating exactly how long those
two items will last me and my daughter.
Somehow, we made it a week with $10 in
grocery money.

I can remember taking ramen noodles and trying
to make them gourmet,
and more than that, I can remember the times
that she ate dinner and I couldn't,
and I told myself that if I just drink enough
water I can convince my stomach that I'm full.

I can remember taking all of my purses out of
the closet and dumping them on the floor and
counting all the loose change, hoping we'd have
enough gas to make it through the weekend.
I remember.
Experiencing lack when you're by yourself is
one thing but it's a whole different ballpark
when you're doing it with the child watching.

I share these stories with you to let you know that I've been there.
I emphasize and I promise you it gets better please don't give up; you'll find the right resources, you'll find the right help you'll find the right jobs, you'll get the right promotions and you and your kids will eventually smile at those old days when you look at how far you've made it.

And yes you will make it!

"Times may be tough but I'm tougher. There is something beautiful on the other side of this journey. My kids and I will have prosperous lives—lives of abundance and overflow. Greater is coming for us!"

On Days It's Hard to Forgive...

On the days it's hard to forgive yourself,
on the days you look back and wonder how you
got here,
remember that life is cumulative.
Every second, every minute, every day is
leading up to something valuable and priceless,
every lesson we learn makes us wiser, stronger,
better.

So yes you've had some mistakes, some
mishaps, some missteps but it's not a failure if
you learned something!
What can you learn from these moments? What
wisdom can you give to your children from
these moments.
We do a great job of forgiving everybody else
but it's only fair if we do the work to forgive
ourselves too.

*"I am not my past, I am not my mistakes; these
things didn't break me, only built me, fortified
me, it made me stronger. I'm getting better every
day. As much as I forgive others, I also forgive
myself. I am not my past."*

On the Days You're Struggling to Be Yourself Again

Sometimes you just see the reminder of who you are, who you were before these little creatures came into your life.

You need a reminder of who you are.

You are a person before them and you'll be a person after them.

They call you mommy but the name that's on your driver's license is something different.

Who are you when the name mommy isn't being called or better yet who would you like to be?

Work toward finding that place and then walking into it!

Who are you? Who do you want to be?

"I have a lot of titles and mommy is not the only one, I am an individual who enjoys my hobbies and my pastimes. I could be both a mommy and a person. I know who I am and I love who I am, both with my kids and in times away from them, I know who I am and I love who I am."

Lexi's Sticky Note 12/2/2023

29

Of course I'll make it happen, that's what moms do.

Of course I'll slay the day, that's what moms do.

I may need a coffee IV but I'm stepping up to the plate with all I got and I'm determined to knock it out the park.

YOU ARE A SUPERHERO!

Your cape may be invisible but we see it and we know it's there!

Your superpowers? Well they include springing into action whenever someone scrapes their knee, supersonic hearing, and the ability to juggle at all with ease.
You are a superhero.

You may not be out here fighting crime but you're fighting running noses and avoiding stepping on legos on the floor, which is a feat all by itself
You're teaching your kids how to share how to listen, by being both a disciplinarian and a nurturer.
You made the food and finances stretch.

Who could do that except a superhero? You've got lightning speed and we know because as soon as they scream mom, you make it to them, in an instant. You are a superhero, no one else can do what you do.

And for the most part mom, you're doing it on
your own. So on the days that you don't feel
good enough remind yourself how credibly
super you are,
how incredibly powerful you are,
how amazing you are that you didn't give up
when you could have and you are still showing
up everyday
You are a superhero.